Minimalism

for a Fulfilling and Meaningful Life

Anthony Glenn

Copyright © 2020 Anthony Glenn

All rights reserved.

ISBN: 9798636144960

Table of Contents

Introduction 5

We Seek Happiness in the Wrong Places 7

What Too Much Stuff Does to Us and How It Distracts Us from What's Important 9

What is Minimalism? 13

How Minimalism Affects One's Life 14

The Most Important Ingredient of Minimalism: Intention 17

Decide on Your WHY: Your Priorities, What You Want, and What to Let Go 19

Rules of Minimalism: Where to Start? 21

Simplify Your Wardrobe 26

Declutter Your Digital Life 32

How to Get Rid of Paper Clutter 37

How Minimalism Can Impact Your Workout Routine 41

A Minimalistic Diet 44

How to Pack for Travel as a Minimalist 47

Minimalism for Productivity 50

Create a Minimalistic Schedule 53

Conclusion and a Bit More About my Story 55

Introduction

Ten years ago, I was living the life I was always meant to. Actually, it was the only way I could imagine how my life should be. I graduated from university, got a job with an excellent salary. I was proud and satisfied. Then I bought my first car and a fantastic apartment. I worked even harder to earn the trust of my employers. The long hours paid off, I got a promotion, and my finances grew. I was now able to afford even better stuff and a luxurious lifestyle, but I was also spending four to five hours more in the office each day. I didn't care. I had everything I wanted, and while my friends were getting married and having babies and struggling to pay all their bills and living expenses, I could relax. I had everything others could only dream of. Moreover, I could help them with that. I was sure I didn't want to travel with only a backpack like my friend Joshua, or to neglect my brilliant career to play with kids like Matthew. I assured myself everything was perfect.

Except it was not. It hit me like a hurricane. I suddenly realized the complete emptiness of my life. I was working all day long, even nights when needed, to "build a better life." Then I bought stuff, expecting it to bring me joy and satisfaction, only to find myself working even harder to keep it and obtain more. It was never enough and I hardly had any time to enjoy anything my money made possible for me. I was chasing more. Yes, I could travel anywhere on earth. But I couldn't leave my job for a single day. I could help my friends and family with financial issues, but they slowly gave up on me. I waited for more than a week for someone to call me, and no one did. Not even my parents. And I wasn't angry, I was ashamed. I was the one who never "had time" to talk to mom or to go to coffee with friends. I still hadn't seen my newborn nephew for God's sake and the kid had already turned two!

All that hit me hard and left me crushed. I realized I didn't have a life outside the office. I had the job that paid for many, many expensive and beautiful things that couldn't make me any less lonely. They couldn't help me with the overwhelming anxiety they raised. They couldn't bring people back to my life. That was the first time I went on vacation after many years of being available at work 24/7—and it was also the first time I didn't care. Things had to change. And it demanded time alone in silence. That was the point when I changed my life and the summer when I discovered minimalism. From then on, my life was never the same again.

We Seek Happiness in the Wrong Places

As a society, we are assured that material possesions are necessary for a happy life. Only when all of our needs are met can we enjoy life. Sure, there is a logic in that, but where is the limit? When is it enough? When will you finally permit yourself to do what truly matters if you have thousands of needs, both real and the fake ones? If you believe you really need everything you see in commercials, you'll never get there. It's like a never-ending race. It's never enough, it's never done, and you will never be free.

So we learn to find joy in material stuff. We make shopping our hobby and afford ourselves little sparks of endorphin with every new package. It's enough to spend a few hours in a shopping mall or just a click, and you get a fresh dose of happiness. But unfortunately that feeling doesn't last long. You'll be left empty again, craving more.

Well, maybe happiness lies in bigger things, we think. I'll be happy when I sit in my brand new car or when I step into my new dream home. But guess what? The endorphin jumps are almost the same as those when you buy a new pair of shoes. They leave you disappointed again. Maybe it should be an even bigger house, you think. So you need to work longer hours, not seeing your kids, your spouse, your parents, or friends. You put off life for later. But that later often doesn't ever come. This truth made me feel frightened, anxious, sad, mad, and finally, thankful. I'm grateful I realized it in time to change my life.

What I know for sure is that happiness is not hidden in more stuff, better stuff, more expensive stuff. It's not in material stuff at all. Chasing after them is the sure way to never find true happiness, meaning, and inner peace.

What Too Much Stuff Does to Us and How It Distracts Us from What's Important

What's wrong with having a lot of possessions? What's wrong in working hard for high compensation? you ask.

Nothing, at first glance. It's wonderful to live comfortably, to have everything you need or want, to be able to help others, and never worry about money again. Until it's not. If you work as much as you have to for the cash you need in order to afford yourself and your loved ones things that make life easier and bring it value, that's perfectly fine. The thing is, most of us don't know when it's enough. We work as much as we can to earn as much as we can to buy, buy, buy. We accumulate all sorts of things just to show the world we have them so that we can label ourselves "successful."

Some of our belongings serve us, making our everyday life comfortable, easier, or nicer. And they should all be there. But there are also things that don't bring any value to our lives. We buy and keep them for the wrong reasons. If you don't use an item, don't like it, don't have space for it, if it doesn't bring value to your life, in a word, it's clutter. Although past generations would see nothing wrong in having too much stuff "just in case," you might not be aware of the fact that your clutter is not good for you at all.

All those things that pile up in the corner, all the junk in your drawers, also your digital clutter, and all the unchecked items in your planner, they all make a mess of your life.

Altogether, they distract you from what truly matters.

Too much stuff makes you a slave. You become captive to your belongings. All those things you gathered, believing they would make you happy, need you to devote your time and attention to them. So instead of going out and enjoying a sunny day, you need to dust and vacuum and clean everything that doesn't make you smile. It's nice to have enough space in your home for everything you need, but if you think a bit more about it, do you really enjoy cleaning a huge house you don't need?

It makes it hard to keep focused. It's not easy to maintain a laser focus in a messy, cluttered space. Also, you can't give your undivided attention to a particular task if your to-do list is packed with all sorts of things and you're in a rush to keep up.

Too much stuff makes you stressed, disorganized, and anxious. You might feel trapped and unable to do what is expected of you, so you feel like a failure all the time. No one can win when expectations are so high and you have to handle the task, the subconscious clutter, and the real, physical mess. Too much stuff makes everything harder.

If you tend to procrastinate, excess stuff will support you in that bad habit. You'll always have an excuse to put something off for later. It's always more important to take care of clutter than to finish a task.

Unsolved clutter drains your energy. It keeps your cortisol levels high and makes you exhausted and stressed all the time. It's not good for your health, nor your overall well-being.

Too much stuff consumes your time. Whether it's a pool in your yard, a fancy sports car, too many outfits, gadgets, too much of anything, they require your time. Money will always come back, but our time will not. That's why it's so important how do you spend it. And our most precious memories are never about material stuff. Ever.

Belongings make you attached. When they begin to define you, you are no longer able just to go away. And it's sad because you get an illusion of security, but actually, you lose your freedom.

Finally, too much stuff distracts you from what really matters in life. Instead of thinking about crucial subjects, investing our precious time and energy in happiness, love, people, experiences, we chase money to spend on unimportant stuff that becomes clutter, disrupts our focus, and harms our planet.

What is Minimalism?

Long story short, minimalism is a philosophy that says you only need to focus on basics in everything. You need to possess only what's necessary and to focus only on priorities. Since "basics," "necessary," and "priorities" have different meanings for each person, everyone has their own understanding of minimalism. You can live with only one pair of shoes and one chair in the house, or have 25 forks and three mirrors and still be a minimalist. The point is not in the number of items you possess. It's rather in the mindset and the intention.

You can apply principles of minimalism to anything: belongings, schedules, art, finances, relationships, anything. The main idea is to get rid of everything that stands in our way so we can devote our focus and energy to what truly matters, whatever that is for you.

Being a minimalist doesn't mean you lack anything. It means that everything in your life, whether material or non-material, is there for a reason. It's all there because you consciously choose it to be. It's all about the intention. As long as everything in your life is intentionally there to bring some value, you can consider yourself a minimalist.

How Minimalism Affects One's Life

Once you decide to adopt a minimalist mindset, things will change in many ways.

You'll get more space. Your home will look tidier, breathable, more fresh and clean. You'll realize that you actually have more space than you believed. The thing is, you'll pare it down to what is important enough to hold your space.

You'll also have more free time. We all have the same amount of time, but what differs are our priorities. When you say no to everything you don't enjoy doing, you'll have more time for activities that matter to you.

You'll discover that the time required to clean and tidy your space has shrunk. Fewer belongings demand less work, so you'll have some extra free time and energy you would otherwise spend on chores.

You'll have extra time and energy to do more of what makes you happy, what you truly enjoy. When I stopped working so much and turned to another path, I was shocked to discover what I was missing out on all that time. There were so many far more interesting things to do than sitting in the office. I used to not be able to imagine what today is my reality: hanging out with friends, going swimming, cuddling with my gorgeous spouse, playing on the beach, surfing, reading, inviting friends to dinner for no reason, watching movies. Sounds lazy? Maybe. The old me would be really anxious about it. The new me doesn't care. The point is, whatever you want to do, you can. You just need to decide what is important and what isn't.

Once you know how much you really need, you won't obsess over money. Your spending will go down because you don't have to pay for unimportant stuff. You don't engage in the rat race anymore. So you need less money to support yourself—and no, you don't need to have the best car on the street.

All of this will significantly reduce your stress levels. You'll become peaceful beyond your expectations. Can you imagine how beneficial it is for your overall health? Your body, mind, and soul will thank you for freeing them from that horrible aggressor: stress.

You'll become a better son, better spouse, father, uncle, friend. And you will enjoy your meaningful relationships. Relationships are a crucial part of our lives, and they need to be nurtured. When you free yourself from unneeded ballast, choose who truly brings value to your life and give them your undivided attention. The relationships will grow and bloom, multiplying happiness.

Your health will also experience benefits from your new minimalistic mindset. Not only will your body thank you for reduced stress and also a reduced number of allergens in your home, but your mental health will also celebrate. Anxiety will decrease and you'll notice an improvement in clarity and ability to focus. From that point, when you intentionally focus on something you want to accomplish, you'll find it easier to concentrate, be productive, and achieve your goals.

With all that in mind it's not surprising that, in the end, minimalism will bring you a lot of joy and happiness.

Everybody wants to know their life has meaning and purpose. We all want to live in alignment with our values, to have inner peace, and experience balance in all areas. Minimalism can help with all of that.

Today, I can say that all this happened in my life. It changed dramatically, and I'm endlessly thankful I adopted a minimalist mindset in time to enjoy numerous long-term benefits.

The Most Important Ingredient of Minimalism: Intention

We've already stated that intention is the most significant characteristic of minimalism. It requires you to define your intentions and then organize everything around them. Think for a while about what you want in life—what you want to do, with whom, where, how you want your home to look, how you want to feel, what to experience, what you want others to think of you, what you want to gift the world. Then think about how your current situation fits into this picture. Decide which areas of your life will most dramatically impact your whole life. That is the area that needs your focus at the beginning. Decide on your most important values and most significant goals and dreams.

Once you have a clear vision of the life you want, you can clearly see what is sufficient in your current reality. It's time to start freeing your life from everything that's not in alignment with your values, whether it's clothes, furniture, digital trash, people who make you feel bad, your negative beliefs and thoughts, everything that keeps you from being happy and getting where you want.

What's crucial is that you do it intentionally, that you have a clear intention to live a certain way.

What you decide to remove from your life has to be removed intentionally. What you decide needs to remain, stays intentionally in order to make your life easier and better.

Decide on Your WHY: Your Priorities, What You Want, and What to Let Go

If you don't want to give up halfway when it becomes challenging, you need to be clear about your why. So, why do you want a change? What is it about your current life that is not in alignment with your values? What do you hope to gain from turning to minimalism? It might be more free time, more time with your loved ones, for hobbies, more clarity, more peace of mind, better focus, higher productivity, more contributions, purpose, and deeper meaning.

Think about your priorities. Choose four to five things that mean the most to you and write them down. What's the crucial ingredient that colors your life? The main goal is to get rid of unnecessary things so you have more to invest in what truly matters. For instance, if you wish to give your loved ones your undivided attention, you need to get rid of unimportant distractors, like notifications on your phone.

As it's important to know what you want to get from minimalism, it's also good to define what you want to let go. For instance, you might want to let go of stress, anger, resentment, anxiety, fears, limiting beliefs, fake friends, activities you don't enjoy, and anything that doesn't bring value to your life.

This was your first step towards your new, minimalistic mindset. Now, it's time to apply principles of minimalism to all segments of your life. Before we start with downsizing, it's good to know some basic rules that can serve you as guide when it's not so easy to decide on certain things.

Rules of Minimalism: Where to Start?

You want to adopt minimalism as your lifestyle, but where to begin?

There are no right or wrong answers. Some people start by unfriending people on Facebook, others by throwing out unnecessary items from the basement. Some sell their huge houses and cars, while some declutter their junk drawer. In other words, you choose where to begin.

However, the most common way to begin is by decluttering. In getting rid of clutter, you'll see the results fastest, your home will change, and it will be obvious. There are few things more liberating than seeing bags of clutter leave your space. That will boost your motivation to keep on with changes and it's easy because it doesn't require serious hard decisions: if you don't need it, it's clutter. Clutter must go, the end. You have far fewer belongings and you can think of yourself as a minimalist.

Decide if it's clutter. If yes, it has to go. But first, let's define what clutter means. In short, it's everything you have but don't use, don't like, or don't have a place for. It doesn't have to be broken, dirty, or torn. It can be an expensive item in perfect condition, yet not useful to you. The main idea is to only keep things that add value to your life. It might be useful, beautiful, make you feel good. If none those are the case, it's clutter. So for each item, ask yourself: Do I use it? Do I like it? Does it have its place? If yes, keep it. If not, toss it.

Don't keep duplicates. This is a super-simple trick to speed up your decluttering process. Nobody can wear two pairs of sunglasses at the same time, two swimsuits, or things like that. Sure, you need to have enough clothes to wear something clean every day and enough plates for yourself, your family, and guests. But there are other sorts of things where no one needs more than one. Put all the duplicates in a donation box.

Quality over quantity is one of the fundamental principles of minimalism. It's a highly eco-friendly concept. You don't want to go shopping every other week or to keep things in case others break. Once you've decided you don't need a ton of stuff, you'll have enough money to invest in high-quality items. Make it a rule always to choose quality and you'll never need quantity again.

Decide how many items of a particular kind you need when it comes to the need for multiples—shirts, for example. I've found that other's formulas don't work perfectly for me here, so I counted how many shirts I actually need. For me, it goes like this: I wear a clean shirt every day and I do the laundry once a week. So that's seven. Then, I work out four times a week. That's 11. I also sleep in a T-shirt and I wear one shirt for two nights. That's how we come to 14 shirts in my closet. Is this too much? No, it's enough for me. Can I be a minimalist if I have 14 T-shirts? Absolutely! I know why I decided to have 14 of them. Some say you have to possess under 100 things to be considered a minimalist. This is nonsense, if you ask me. I don't care if you have 56 forks, as long as you know why and you use them all. So do some math for yourself and decide how many items of each sort you need.

Do you use it? If you don't use an item, you obviously don't need it. But I *am* going to use it! Yes, I know. Did you use it in the last year? Will you do it in the next year? If yes, keep it. If not, pass it on to someone who really does goes camping, cooks, paints, etc. Don't keep things for your imagined life, something you think you should be doing. Those things won't make you do it, nor will they do it by themselves. What they really do is occupy space in your home.

You don't owe anyone to keep anything. We all have stuff we've gotten from others like presents, or they passed their clutter on to us. We feel as if we're supposed to save it forever. But you don't have to. You shouldn't be trapped by everything everyone gives you, and you don't have to feel guilty if you toss that ugly sweater you got from your aunt. Those things don't represent the people who gave them to us, and tossing them doesn't mean you don't appreciate the person. It just means you don't want to be trapped by clutter.

Detach yourself from material things. They represent nothing. The truth is in modern society we are all convinced that our possessions represent who we are. That's why it is hard to let them go. It's time to realize that your stuff doesn't represent who you are. It doesn't show how good of a person you are, how kind, generous, creative, or anything else. What these things do represent is what you choose to buy. That's all. Your belongings don't define you in any way. They just represent themselves and what you bought.

Clutter can't come back. Without this rule, your decluttering process is a waste of time and energy. What you once decided to discard must be tossed or donated. It can't come back into your house.

Everything needs its home. What you decide to keep has to have its place. Decide and declare an official home for everything, even the tiniest item that you decide to keep. That's the recipe for a tidy, organized home. Once you have fewer things and each of them has its place, it will be super-easy to keep perfect order and enjoy the benefits of minimalism.

Don't take on too much at once. I know you're excited and you want to do it all at once to finally see a change. But if you are too motivated and you rush to do everything at once, you are at high risk of giving up. It becomes too much and you lose all your enthusiasm. Taking baby steps to continue making progress is a far better recipe for success. In the end, minimalism is all about having less, but with intention and high quality. Apply those principles to the process too. Be a real minimalist from the beginning. It's better to declutter only a drawer and then sit on the floor and drink a cup of tea in silence, enjoying it, than rushing to downsize all of your belongings at once and stress out about it.

Stay intentional, mindful, and enjoy freeing up space, time, and energy. It's a process, not a single task. It's a journey, not a destination. Enjoy it, breathe deeply, and stay mindful about your transformation, aware of the effect it has on you. Have fun and remember why you began in the first place. Take a look at your written priorities and intentions. This will give you a boost of motivation whenever you don't feel enthusiastic.

Simplify Your Wardrobe

Is your closet full, packed with stuff you don't wear, don't like, or can't wear because it's torn or stained? Do you have to spend your mornings in front of the closet, thinking and stressing out about what to wear, how it fits and looks, what others will think of you? This was the case with me. I used to spend my mornings stressing out about it and wasting my precious energy on meaningless things like that. Even now many years later, I declutter my wardrobe every six months or so. I know it's time for downsizing when it becomes hard to find stuff or I see there are many things I don't wear.

Unless you live under a rock, you have probably heard people mention how they edited their wardrobe and how it has changed their lives. You've probably also heard about some terrifically successful rich people who wear the same outfit every day. Although it might sound too New Age, it's surprisingly true how the condition of your wardrobe impacts the quality of your life.

If you go through your clothes, you'll most likely notice that 20% to even 80% of it is stuff you don't use. When I decluttered my wardrobe for the first time, there was only a teeny tiny percent of the stuff I loved to wear. And guess what? I could hardly ever wear it because it was in the laundry basket too often. I also never had enough socks and underwear, so I had to do laundry more often than I planned. Meanwhile, the doors of my closet couldn't close because of the overflowing stuff I didn't use. Then one day, a lightbulb went on above my head. Why couldn't I have many of my same favorite T-shirt? Why couldn't I wear my favorite outfit every day?

And that is what exactly I did. I bought many of the same items that I love, like my favorite gray shirt, and threw out the rest.

Since then, I truly enjoy my simple, minimalistic wardrobe. Before I tell you what I own exactly, as an example of what can be enough for a man, I want to share a few benefits I experienced:

- I don't waste my time standing in front of the closet each morning, thinking about what to pick.
- I don't struggle anymore about what fits and looks good.
- I don't stress anymore about what others will think of me based on my outfit. I'm sure I have a lot to offer and it's worth my casualness and simplicity.
- I don't waste my time shopping. I've never enjoyed spending time in malls and shops.
- I finally have enough socks and underwear.

- I have much less stress.
- I learned that nobody cares about what you wear. People think about themselves and their own looks.

Here's my ultimate wardrobe list that can serve as an example. It might be different for you, so be free to edit it in any way to meet your needs. Remember, possessing more than this won't make you less of a minimalist!

1. My favorite go-to T-shirt: 10 in a light color, 10 in a dark color
2. A pair of jeans
3. Everyday summer shorts
4. 2 comfy shorts for wearing only around the house
5. 5 pairs of gym shorts
6. 2 tank tops
7. 1 pair of colored pants
8. 2 button-down shirts
9. 1 suit for special occasions
10. 1 hoodie
11. 20 pairs of underwear
12. 10 pairs of socks
13. 1 sweatshirt
14. 1 sweater
15. 1 jacket
16. a watch
17. a belt

18. 1 beanie hat
19. 1 pair of everyday sneakers
20. 1 pair of gym sneakers
21. 1 pair of fancy shoes
22. 1 pair of boots
23. 1 pair of flipflops

You see, it's more than enough. Sure, I don't possess everything I could ever need, but if I travel somewhere where I need a sky suit, for example, I can borrow one. The same goes for all the things for special conditions. It's better to borrow or buy a second-hand item than to have it taking up space in my closet for the whole year, just in case.

Now, here is some advice on how to edit your wardrobe, to turn from messy to minimalistic and put your mind at ease.

Pull out everything in your closet and place it on the bed or on a sheet on the floor. Then go through the pile, deciding what stays and what goes.

Put all of the stuff that doesn't fit anymore in a pile for donating. If you want to lose some weight, nice. But when you lose it, buy some new, better fitting clothes. Until then, it's just taking up space.

Everything you haven't worn for more than a few months, put in the donation pile. You will probably never wear those items again.

Discard everything stained and damaged beyond repair. If you can sew it, do it the next day. Resist the urge to save all of the torn or stained clothes to wear around the house, otherwise you'll end up with a full closet and nothing to wear.

If an item doesn't match anything you own or it's out of style, donate it. Of course, keep it if you still wear it.

If you live somewhere where you have both warm and cold times of year, put seasonal clothes in a container and label it. There's no point in keeping it in your closet all year round.

When you're in doubt about an item, put it in a special container, out of sight. If you ever want to wear it, take it out. If you don't need it in a few months, it's time to donate it.

Make comfort your priority
When you choose clothes to keep, remember that comfort is more important than looks. Clothes should serve you, not the other way round. The goal is not to have to think about clothes but to be free to focus on other things.

Mix and match
Try to only keep things that can be combined in various ways. When your clothes are in the same color scheme, you don't have to worry about what

goes with what. The best colors for mixing and matching are white and black, gray, dark blue, and khaki. Toss in some color once in a while and you'll be all set. For instance, jeans are great for mixing and matching. You can pair them with any shirt and you'll look put together.

From now on, make decluttering a regular event. Even if you are not a shopaholic, stuff accumulates in our closets over time. It's good to check on what you use every so often and see what's merely taking up space.

Declutter Your Digital Life

Have you ever had a situation where your computer tells you there's no more space on the hard disc? Or where you want to take a photo, but you're out of storage space on your phone, so you frenetically go through your pictures and delete them randomly? When you can finally take a photo, the moment is gone. Since we live in a digital space, our digital clutter, junk files, and unused applications are also things that pile up if we don't take care of them. Although this clutter won't stand in your way physically, it has the same impact on your life as any other kind. However, our digital clutter is often something we put off until it can't be ignored anymore.

If you want to adopt a minimalistic lifestyle, you need to apply it to your digital life as well. Here we'll talk about all of it—from your phone and applications to photos, videos, documents, and your inbox. The main goal is to become more intentional about how you use media and technology.

Declutter your documents. Go through and delete all of the documents you no longer need. Treat your desktop the same way as your physical desktop. You wouldn't keep piles of paper on it, would you? It should be nice and clean, so keep only what you use at least on a weekly basis. While deciding what to keep and what to send to the recycle bin, avoid "just in case" syndrome. You need it or you don't. Not "just, maybe, if."

Once you've deleted everything that you don't need or use, archive and organize the files that you've decided to keep.

Make lean and simple solutions for documents that you often use. You should also find some backup solutions. This may be an external hard disc or in the cloud.

You'll notice that the majority of stuff that takes up storage space are videos and images. No matter how many of them you have, weed them. Delete all the duplicates and unnecessary pictures and videos. Keep only those you actually like and want to keep. Store them in a safe place, the cloud, or an external hard drive. Otherwise, if something happens to your computer, you will regret it and be very sad you've lost them.

When it's about photos on your phone, it's the same case. Send all of them to the computer and securely store them.

Manage the applications on your phone. All the apps you haven't used for six months or more, you can delete. If you ever need them, you can always reinstall and uninstall them again.

Clean up your social media. If you are one of those people who unintentionally scroll down the status feeds and waste time looking at a bunch of things you don't care about, it's time to do something. Unfriend and unfollow profiles and pages, leave groups you don't care about. Ask yourself: would I wish a happy birthday to this person? If yes, you should be friends on Facebook or Instagram. If not, you shouldn't have them as virtual "friends."

Deal with your inbox. It can seem like a wild, out of control beast. Unsubscribe from emails that you won't open and read. For all the email you get, try to take action immediately. Archive it, reply, do what is needed, and move it from your inbox to where it belongs. Ideally, you should reach zero in your inbox, which means that you don't have anything there. You wouldn't let your physical mail pile up in the mailbox. Treat your digital inbox the same way.

An awesome thing I like to practice every so often is that every time I notice I'm becoming too glued to my phone, I do a digital detox. I sometimes practice it for seven days, sometimes for two weeks, or even a month. The goal is to become more intentional about using media, and the benefits are numerous. Every time I notice I'm more conscious, centered, focused, and relaxed. The rules for the detox are pretty simple:

- Schedule all your email activity for once a day. All the checking, answering, and whatever you have to do with email, do it at a certain time each day. The rest of the day, resist the urge to check your inbox.
- Limit your social media time to half an hour a day. There's no point in mindlessly scrolling down Facebook or Instagram.
- Limit all streaming to one hour daily. Here I think of YouTube, Netflix, podcasts, whatever you like to watch or listen to.
- Customize notifications so they don't distract you.
- Keep all the screens out of your bedroom. Your sleep will improve without the blue light from your phone and if you share a bed with a significant other, your partner will be glad too.

These are some general rules I follow each time I need to detoxify from technology and too much information. This might work for you or it might not. So I encourage you to develop your own rules for a digital diet and find out what will work best for you.

What I realized practicing this is that social media doesn't make me more connected. I was scared at first that something might go wrong if I took a break, but nothing collapsed and my relationships never suffered from taking a digital detox. I feel much happier and experience more contentment. Also, I am far more productive and focused. This all helps me create a healthy relationship with technology and use it for the highest good.

Of course, nothing's wrong with a little TV, social media, and other passive entertainment at the end of a busy day. But it's important to set a limit and maintain it.

How to Get Rid of Paper Clutter

Do you remember the fresh, light feeling when you first moved into your home? There were so many options. And there were no papers anywhere. But six months is enough for piles of paper to build up.

Maybe you moved in only six months ago and you have a small pile of paper clutter on your counter, or perhaps you have a monumental collection of paper gained from over ten years. The process is the same, just its length will be different. Although it might feel daunting to even look at all those piles, don't let that discourage you and make you give up before you start. Here's a guide on how to declutter paper once and for all. No minimalist hoards paper clutter.

For this purpose, you will need three empty containers or boxes.

Most of the papers you have been keeping for years will be discarded in the end—you will never file or organize them. So you'll dispose of a lot of stuff and the first box, the recycle bin, should be the biggest one.

The second box is for the papers you should keep and that will be the smallest amount.

The third one is meant for all of those "I'm not sure about this" papers. Put as few papers as you can here, then label it with the date when the box should be discarded without opening, and place it somewhere out of sight. Set the re-examination date for three or six months. If it happens that you need something from it during that time, you know it's still there and can simply take it out. If you don't take back anything, just toss the whole box.

Sort all of the papers into one of those categories by deciding for each item if it is easy, medium, or hard to replace. If it's super-easy to replace, you can get a new one or you can find information online or with a phone call and you don't need to keep it.

If a paper can be replaced, but you need to take some action that could take a while, about 15 minutes or so, it's medium replaceable.

And if it's something unique, like tax papers or a marriage or birth certificate, or guarantees, definitely keep it. File it all in one place.

Let's get to some realistic examples:

Birthday cards: It's really kind of your loved ones to show you attention this way. Appreciate them, be thankful, but this doesn't mean you are supposed to keep all of the cards. You will get new ones next year. The exceptions are cards from dear people who are not here anymore. In that case, display the item.

Owner's manuals: Today, you can find all the information you could need online. It's more likely you will search for a certain piece of information on the internet than that you will ever read the manual. Not to mention the owner manuals in many different languages you get when you buy something big.

Insurance: Life insurance, health insurance, car insurance—whatever you need about insurance, you can make a phone call. It's more efficient than trying to find information in those papers. Toss them.

Magazines: If you are one of those people who actually reads magazines, enjoy them. But if that unopened magazine on your coffee table makes you feel guilty, get rid of it. If you ever have so much free time to wish you had magazines, you can always buy them or borrow from a friend or the local library.

Notes from conferences and seminars: These might be particularly useful and full of quality information. However, if haven't read these notes and they're over a year old, you don't need to keep them. They might be outdated or you can find them online.

Bills and receipts: If it's out of date, throw it away. There's no point in keeping a bill in case of returning an item that's already used.

Coupons: If you collect coupons, don't let them fly all around the house. Decide on a special place for them. It's best to keep them in your car so you can use them when you go shopping. From time to time, toss the expired ones.

And that's it. You have probably emptied the trash can a few times up to this point. File those important papers you need to keep, put the "maybe" box out of sight, and be merciless about new papers coming into your house.

How Minimalism Can Impact Your Workout Routine

Principles of minimalism can be applied to all aspects of life and can affect all the areas of your life. Exercising is not an exception. I've noticed that since I became a minimalist, my workout routine changed in terms of being more focused, more intentional, and consistent.

Here we'll talk about how to apply main minimalism concepts to exercise.

Be intentional.
First, decide on your goals, what you want to achieve by exercising. Then decide on the right approach and make a proper workout plan with help from the internet or a personal trainer. Your workout routine will be different if you want to build muscle mass, strengthen your body, prepare for a marathon, or lose weight.

Be laser-focused for the best results with the least effort.
I used to do all the muscle groups in each session. Needless to say, my training was too long and hard and I would give up my routine after some time. Now, I work out only for 30 minutes a day and I do only one muscle group a day. For instance:

Day 1 - biceps
Day 2 - triceps
Day 3 - back
Day 4 - chest
Day 5 - legs
Day 6 - glutes
Day 7 - rest

This works great for me. Try out different options and find your perfect routine that requires less effort and time in a gym, yet gives you the desired results.

Take it slowly.
Don't speed things up and don't try to impress anyone by lifting more than you can. Not only will you look like a dummy, but you can hurt yourself too. Begin with easy exercises and small weights, then progress gradually. That's the only healthy way. Otherwise, you'll burn out at the beginning and then spend weeks recovering. That's not the way to build a healthy habit.

Be consistent.
It's better to exercise for 20 minutes every day than to train for two hours on a weekend.

You don't need fancy equipment.
Working out is not a reason to create fake needs. Your own weight is usually enough. You can even do most of the exercises using a block of wood in a

forest. If you go to a gym, great for you. That's enough.

Choose the activity you enjoy.
Don't force yourself to run or to go to the gym just because it's mainstream and you think you are supposed to that. Try out different things, go swimming, biking, hiking, group sports, until you find out what you enjoy the most.

A Minimalistic Diet

This might sound weird, as if you should be hungry all the time. But actually, the minimalistic approach can help you with a healthy diet too. If you apply these principles to your diet, you'll never be obese, and you'll feel healthy and energized. At least, this was true in my case. I hadn't been overweight, but my body wasn't in perfect shape and I had a few pounds more than I needed. That completely changed when I adopted my new lifestyle. Not only did I begin a new habit of working out, but I also changed my diet a lot.

Applying the main principles of minimalism to food means that you keep in your diet only real food that nourishes your body and spirit. You don't need processed sugar, soda, or junk food of any kind. Today, my diet is simple and clean: I eat a lot of fresh fruit and vegetables, poultry, fish, nuts, and seeds. And I find it's completely enough. I don't need sweets (except fruit and moderate amounts of honey), dairy, food in plastic packaging, or anything my grandpa wouldn't recognize. If it grows, have at it. If your great-grandparents would know its name, eat it. If not—you don't need it.

I've noticed that we as a society eat a lot for all kinds of reasons: when we're hungry, thirsty, upset, nervous, bored, emotionally hungry, or even if there's just a piece of something delicious available. I decided to keep only one good reason to eat: hunger. So I only eat when I feel hungry. All my other needs have to be met some other way. It required some practice and introspection, but after some time I learned to recognize my needs and fulfill them.

Your diet should be simple and your meals should not require a lot of time to prepare. Eating is not the main activity in life, but the fuel for other, more interesting things. So you need quality fuel to run your vehicle, not another complicated activity that absorbs crazy amounts of your time. Your food should serve you, not the other way round. Also, it's not wise to put vast amounts of food into your body, making it overweight, and then putting extra time and effort into making it looks better. You have to spend a lot of time and energy in the slimming process. And that's not the worst part. If you practice an unhealthy lifestyle, what awaits you sooner or later are health issued and medical help. Do you know how much energy, stress, and money that requires? It's not pleasant at all. Think about your health while you still have it. It should be one of your priorities, and what you do every day towards that goal counts.

Of course, every now and then you can eat some "junk food." You don't want to entirely have to give up small treats, dinner with friends, french fries with kids after a movie. But now those are exceptions, and I focus on the taste and enjoyment rather than just gulping down the meal. In the end, taste and pleasure are the only reasons why I eat some unhealthy but delicious bites from time to time.

How to Pack for Travel as a Minimalist

One of the main intentions in minimalism is to be free to see the world, to gain experiences, and make friends instead of buying and hoarding more and more stuff. So once you have more time and money, you will be able to travel more often.

I remember how packing for a trip used to be stressful for me. Now every time I pack for a trip, I feel thankful I'm a minimalist.

Besides the reduced hustle when you are a minimalist, packing for a trip is always a little experiment. You have to ask yourself what you use, what you don't, what are your essential needs, and what are the fake ones. I always ask myself if I really need a thing and what is the worst scenario that might happen if I don't have it with me. It turns out I have very few irreplaceable, essential items. I also don't pack anything heavy because I like to travel light and feel free. I plan my baggage according to the amount of time I plan to spend on the trip, and if I need a bit of extra space, I usually roll all of my clothing instead of just folding it into the suitcase.

What I have discovered over time is also that it's handy to have a quality bag, a rucksack, or a backpack with many dividers and zips on both sides. If I pack well, I can easily reach whatever I need without turning all my stuff upside down.

Just as an example, here is a list of what I pack for a seven-day trip:

- a passport
- wallet
- keys
- sunglasses
- laptop
- my phone
- camera
- ear pads or headphones
- battery charger
- notebook and a pen
- beauty trimmer and razors
- toiletries (for shaving, shower, toothcare)
- five T-shirts
- button-down shirt
- shorts or a pair of pants or jeans
- casual shorts or pants
- swimsuit
- tanktop
- underwear (8 pairs)
- socks (8 pairs)
- jacket
- sneakers

Again, this is just an example. What you pack for a seven-day trip might be different than what I need. I encourage you to adjust your list to your needs. And if you travel with two bags, that's still completely fine. Minimalism should fit with your needs, not the other way around.

Minimalism for Productivity

What does productivity mean to you? In our society, it usually refers to finishing as much as possible and getting the best results with the least input and effort. And that's nice, but what is overlooked here is balance. Productivity is not about finishing a crazy number of tasks in a day. It's about developing sustainable systems and creating a balanced life you can keep up with.

A common mistake is to think that minimalism excludes any ambition. People often imagine a minimalist as one who just sits still and watches the world go round. That couldn't be further from the truth. It's not about giving up on any ambition. It's about finding your true passion and eliminating the rest.

Once you discover what drives you and can define the clear vision of the life you want, you can apply minimalistic principles to the small things that you do every day, to the major systems that take up most of your days.

Set your priorities. If you constantly strive for more work and more money, you'll end up with less—less time for family and relationships, less mental health and happiness. Minimalism teaches us to choose and decide what truly matters. So define your list of priorities and devote some time and energy to each of them, one at a time. Drop all of the tasks that don't support your priorities. It's easier said than done, but you can do it. You just need to be disciplined and keep your priorities in mind.

Stay organized. Use everything that can help you: to-do lists, calendars, notes. That way, you free up space in your memory for more important tasks. Whenever possible, create and implement productive systems. For instance, you can have systems for storing your files, for processing your email, even for the same kinds of projects. They can all have a similar structure and you can have a system that leads you through tasks instead of reinventing one for each task.

First things first. Whatever you are doing, focus first on the biggest things, the foundation and structure, and save the polish for the very end. That way, you'll save yourself a lot of time and effort.

Define where the most stress is coming from. Write down everything that stresses you out. The things that stress you out most should be fixed first.

Stay focused and reduce distractions. The main reason most of us are often not as productive as we would like is that we are constantly distracted by all sorts of things. We live in a world where every activity is disrupted by sounds of notifications.

Don't let others (dis)organize your time and technology dictate your activities. Turn off all notifications while you're doing something, and schedule all social media for a certain time block in a day.

Don't push yourself too hard. The other side of productivity is burnout. Yet if you give yourself space to breathe, creativity recovers, your energy recharges, and you can be more productive and efficient.

Create a Minimalistic Schedule

If you can't find time for savoring life, your schedule is fully packed with everything and anything, it's time to change something. Your capacities are limited, so you can't manage everything and get everywhere. You have to choose again. Pick only the activities that you love or you really have to do because they are closely connected to your goals and priorities. There is always a way to politely refuse things that drain your energy and waste your time. You have to say "no" to all those meaningless conversations, boring formal visits, coffee with someone you don't like, so you can say "yes" to everything that makes you happy and fulfilled. It might be spending time with your family, doing awesome things with friends, enjoying new experiences, expressing yourself through art or a hobby, investing in your career, whatever needs your attention and brings more meaning and sense to your life.

The easiest way to create your minimalistic schedule is to pick only a few things to complete in a day—only as many as you can achieve without sacrificing balance, your inner peace, and enjoyment of little moments that life is made of. Write down all the tasks you have to finish, then decide which of them are important, and which require an emergent action. Your top priority for the day should be an emergent and important task. Finish it first thing in the morning and you'll feel as if you have already won. Then go to other, less important or less emergent tasks.

Leave some empty space between tasks and activities. Don't just jump from one to another without any time to smell the roses. I like to leave my afternoons and evenings totally free from any obligations, and finish everything in the morning and the first half of a day. Adjust your schedule to your needs and preferences, and you'll feel a huge sense of relief. Minimalism is all about focusing on essentials and dropping everything else. When you apply that principle to your schedule, you'll begin to enjoy life more and stress out less.

Conclusion and a Bit More About my Story

I explained at the beginning how I was stuck in an overwhelming office job that was consuming all my energy and time. And it got to the point where I felt completely drained and empty. That was when I realized enough was enough, and so I went on a long-deserved vacation. That was when I discovered minimalism, among some other methods of self-development that helped me a lot. I spent a whole month thinking about my life, my priorities, my life mission, imagining the life I wanted to live. When I came back from that trip, it's not an exaggeration to say that I was another person. I made a few crucial decisions.

First of all, I decided to quit my job and give up the career I had been building all my life. It was not in alignment with my values and priorities. At least, it had been fulfilling to me, but I didn't feel good about it anymore. It was like a marriage that is first built on love, but the love had faded. I knew it was time for a new chapter in life. So I went in another direction and committed to my passions: learning, writing, teaching, self-exploring, and developing.

I adopted minimalism as my lifestyle. I sold my huge house and my fancy sports car, moved to another country, bought a smaller apartment, and a beautiful blue bike instead of a car.

Since then, I have found much more enjoyment, contentment, and fulfillment in my life. Now I live the life I always dreamed of. It's not concentrated around any material possessions—those are just things that I use as long as they serve me. Nothing more or less than that.

I'm surrounded by great people, friends, and colleagues. And I found the love of my life. We do our best to arrange our life together according to minimalism. That project has its ups and downs, but we are definitely devoted to one another, not to materialistic stuff. We collect experiences and make memories, not work long hours to spend more time shopping.

Many things and approaches helped me on my way from being a miserable, lonely man to who I am today. Minimalism is one of them. I'm sure it is an important one. That was my way to explore and know myself, to structure my life, and to decide on its direction. It's not about how many forks you have in the drawer. Trying to have only a certain number of things is just as exhausting as living in clutter. It's about knowing what truly matters, focusing on essentials, and learning how to give up everything that doesn't serve and support you and your purpose.

Happiness is not in our belongings, nor do our possessions define us. Those are just things you've bought and they are simply evidence of your purchase. If they serve you, great. Good for you. If they don't, there's no sense in holding onto them. But if you think your value is based on having something or that you have less worth because you don't have it, you're wrong. Your worth doesn't depend on any material things. You can't buy it, sell it, get it as a gift, or discard it. If you have an item, it might be useful or it could be clutter. But it's not a measure of your worth or who you are.

We all have limited resources, limited time and energy. Be wise when deciding what to do with yours. A happy life is made of happy moments. In each moment, you have a choice. Would you like to spend it more in the office, chasing money to buy more stuff, and then spend many other moments of your life taking care of that stuff? Or would you rather spend it hugging and kissing your loved ones, traveling the world, doing what makes you feel alive?

Minimalism enables you to say yes to all those precious things by using the option to say no to things you don't want. It helps you build the muscle for deciding, "Yes, I love this shirt. No, I don't need this bowl. Yes, I'd love to sit in silence with this person. And no thanks, I don't want another coffee with this one." By practicing minimalism, you will learn how to decide on your priorities and keep them present. You'll learn how to be more mindful about how you use your time and energy. You'll learn how to know what truly matters and how to keep your focus on that, eliminating the rest. These are all invaluable skills extremely useful for self-growth and building a joyful, fulfilled life. And it all starts with a good decluttering.

Printed in Great Britain
by Amazon